April

Happy Birthday

Kahlil Gibran's

LITTLE BOOK OF SECRETS

Dear Margeaux,
Thinking of you &
wishing you a new
year with many
joys & blessings
We love you,
May &

Kahlil Gibran's

LITTLE BOOK OF SECRETS

Neil Douglas-Klotz

HAMPTON ROADS

Copyright © 2019
by Neil Douglas-Klotz

All rights reserved. No part of this publication may be reproduced
or transmitted in any form or by any means, electronic or
mechanical, including photocopying, recording, or by any
information storage and retrieval system, without permission
in writing from Red Wheel/Weiser, LLC. Reviewers may quote
brief passages.

Grateful acknowledgement is made to Nicholas Martin for
permission to reprint excerpts from Gibran's play "Iram of
the Pillars" as translated in *The Arabic Plays of Kahlil Gibran*,
Nicholas Martin, editor. Copyright Nicholas R.M. Martin 2015,
reprinted with permission, all rights reserved.

Cover design by Jim Warner
Cover illustration, Maze by Rebecca Campbell, Private Collection/
    Bridgeman Images
Interior by Deborah Dutton
Typeset in ITC Garamond Std

Hampton Roads Publishing Company, Inc.
Charlottesville, VA 22906
Distributed by Red Wheel/Weiser, LLC
www.redwheelweiser.com

Sign up for our newsletter and special offers by going to
www.redwheelweiser.com/newsletter.

ISBN: 978-1-57174-834-8
Library of Congress Cataloging-in-Publication Data available
upon request.

Printed in Canada
MAR

10   9   8   7   6   5   4   3   2   1

FOR THOSE WHO LONG TO HEAR THE SECRET
THAT CANNOT BE SPOKEN.

Contents

2. Secrets of Life and Death 37

3. Life's Ups and Downs 69

4. Secrets of Good and Evil 91

5. Traveling the Inner Path 127

Sources of the Selections 173

Introduction

In the past ninety years, Kahlil Gibran's *The Prophet* has become one of the most read and quoted books in English. Yet a few contemporary critics have labeled it overly simplistic and philosophically lightweight. *The Prophet*, they say, may have appealed to the 60s generation of new age hippies and greeting card factories, but Gibran skates the surface of real spiritual or mystical thought. The selections in this small volume strongly contradict such opinions. Gibran's best writing expresses a deep, authentic, "native" Middle Eastern spirituality, albeit one that bridges ordinary religious boundaries.

These new "little book" collections take a fresh look at Gibran's words and wisdom, taking into account the major influences in his life: his Middle Eastern culture, nature mysticism, and the Arabic language in which he thought. One could easily argue that what the average reader of Gibran in the 1920s found exotic was the way he clearly expressed a region that most regarded as a mystery. Nearly a hundred years later, understanding the Middle Eastern conundrum—especially the way that a very different culture considers the meaning and purpose of life—has moved from the level of a philosophical problem to become a practical matter of everyday survival.

The book before you collects Gibran's words on life's big questions and the mysteries of the spiritual path. The first book in the series collected his writings on life and nature. The second book focused on love and relationships, and the final one will collect his writings on practical wisdom for daily life, both in community and solitude.

Many of Gibran's early writings focus on life's puzzles and riddles—those questions that cause us to stop what we're doing and ask, "why?" Things we at first see as opposites seem upon consideration to complement each other. How could we know what "good" is, for instance, without an exposure to its opposite, which we call "bad?" Could we truly know life without some intuition of death or feel successful without some experience of failure? For those who reflect on life (even a little), questions like these often provide the starting place for a psychological or spiritual search. How can a person hold opposite points of view at the same time? Why don't people act logically, based on facts? What is, in fact, a "fact"? Do I always make important choices in my life based on factual information? Or do I rarely have all of the information before I jump into a new job, a new relationship, or a major move?

We can see an influence of Gibran's early life story on his fascination with such questions. He was uprooted from his native Lebanon at the age of twelve by his mother who brought his siblings and him to the USA in 1895. Like many migrants today, she was escaping a hopeless situation: poverty, a failed marriage, and a husband in prison for embezzling from the government. Gibran experienced a radical disconnection from his relatives and friends in the move to late 19th century urban Boston, a very different culture from that of his childhood. According to Gibran, life in Ottoman-controlled Lebanon was both insular and feudal, with local lords and church officials in an unholy alliance to keep the *fellahin*—the peasants and those who worked the land—in virtual serfdom.

We can imagine that from an early age Gibran began to see things from two points of view—that of the native of rural Lebanon and that of the American city dweller. Seeing from two points of view at the same time, a split awareness, could only be integrated by either taking a higher view or going crazy. Fortunately for Gibran (and us), he was able to do the former, although toward the end of his young life, the attempts to drown his extreme sensitivities in alcohol finally caught up with him.

Gibran found help in his search for balance and meaning in a number of diverse spiritual influences.

First, as I noted in the introductions to the earlier collections, Gibran was raised as a Maronite Christian, an Eastern church allied to the Roman Catholic but which until the 18th century spoke and used in liturgy the Syriac language, related to Jesus' native Aramaic. The Aramaic-speaking churches historically viewed Jesus, the prophet of Nazareth, as a human being, a small-s "son" of God, who uniquely fulfilled his destiny and expressed the divine life in a way open to all of us. In this sense, we could all become "children" of God, that is, of "Sacred Unity" (the literal translation of the Aramaic word for God, *Alaha*, as well as the equivalent Arabic word *Allah*).

For instance, in a selection contained here, Gibran criticizes those who would only worship Jesus, but not try to become like him spiritually:

They would honor the man unknown
  to them.
What consolation is there in a man like
  themselves,
a man whose kindliness is like their own
  kindliness,
a god whose love is like their own love,
and whose mercy is in their own mercy?

They honor not the man, the living man,
the first man who opened his eyes
and gazed at the sun with eyelids
  unquivering.
Nay, they do not know him,
and they would not be like him.

The ideal of God as "unity"—a unity that contains all opposites—unites the various threads of Middle Eastern mysticism that Gibran expresses. Ultimately, there is no "God *and* human beings" or "God *and* nature" in this tradition. There is only God-Unity-One Reality. Ancient Semitic languages (like ancient Egyptian, Hebrew, Aramaic, and Arabic) do not specify various categories that we take for granted, for instance: transcendent vs. immanent; inside vs. outside; past, present, and future, or body, mind, and spirit.

For instance, the word for "spirit" in ancient Hebrew, Aramaic, and Arabic also means literally "breath." So the words translated as "Holy Spirit" in Jesus' Aramaic language, could also be translated "Holy Breath." Gibran expresses this in a saying from "The Garden of the Prophet," contained here:

> You are God's breath even as the wind
> that shall be neither caught nor caged.

Likewise, there is no preposition that means "within" that does not also mean "among." So what is inside me also affects my outer world and vice versa. Again in Jesus' words in his native language, the reign of God is always both within and among us. Gibran returns to this theme repeatedly in his work, particularly in the long poem that concludes his masterful work

Jesus The Son of Man. Much of this poem, entitled originally "A Man from Lebanon Nineteen Centuries Later" is included here.

When you spoke,
your words were
the far-off whisper of their lips,
when those lips should be
kindled with fire.

You laughed for the marrow in their bones
that was not yet ready for laughter.
and you wept for their eyes that yet
    were dry.

Your voice fathered their thoughts
and their understanding.
Your voice mothered their words
and their breath.

We call upon each other,
but in truth we call upon you,
like the floodtide in the spring
of our want and desire,

and when our autumn comes,
like the ebb tide.

It was only due to the later influence of
Platonic philosophy that the idea of the separa-
tion of humanity from God and nature began to
infect the various Middle Eastern religious tradi-
tions, particularly in their institutional forms. For
those closest to nature, the workers on the land
with whom Gibran was raised, the basic unity
was preserved: the idea that "God," while ulti-
mately a mystery, includes nature and humanity.
This does not mean that "we are God," but rather
that "God" unifies all opposites, includes all
seeming paradoxes, and is the permanence that
includes change. Realizing this permanence is
the goal of the mystical seeker in native Middle
Eastern terms.

As Gibran's character Almustafa says of God
in *The Garden of the Prophet:*

Think now, my comrades and beloved, of
a heart that contains all your hearts, a love
that encompasses all your loves, a spirit that

envelops all your spirits, a voice enfolding
all your voices, and a silence deeper than all
your silences, and timeless.

Throughout Gibran's writings we find this
yearning for the permanent, something that can
be relied upon. And throughout his life, Gibran
sought out those who had the same interest and
could offer him keys to life's secrets.

Did Gibran have a spiritual teacher or teach-
ers? He reports several meetings with sages, and
they cannot all be fictional. We know that he
was influenced by various Sufis who, throughout
the Islamic world at his time, mostly lived either
ordinary lives or as hermits. For instance, one of
Gibran's Arabic plays, "Iram of the Pillars," fea-
tures a seeker who visits a woman Sufi mystic in
the desert, who tells him:

Everything in existence resides in your core,
and all of what is in your core resides in
existence.

In a single drop of water are all the secrets of the seas. In a single atom are all the elements of the Earth. In a single motion of thought are all of the motions and laws of the world. (Martin trans. 2015).

We might compare this to the saying of the 13th-century Persian Sufi mystic Mahmud Shabistari:

Penetrate the heart of one drop of water—you'll be flooded by a hundred pure oceans. If you examine carefully a speck of dust, you'll see a million unnameable beings. . . .

Cosmic rays lie hidden in the pupil of my eye, and somehow the center of my heart accommodates the pulse of the cosmos. (Douglas-Klotz trans. 2011, p. 121).

Gibran's universalism—his ability to find truth in many different traditions—also stems from his interest in the Bahai religion. In 1912, he met and painted Abdul Baha, the son of

Bahai founder Baha'ullah. "There were worlds in his soul," reported Gibran, and the meetings inspired him to a new burst of creativity. We find something of this universalist spirituality in many of Gibran's books, including *Jesus The Son of Man*:

> Many times the Christ has come to the world, and he has walked many lands. And always he has been deemed a stranger and a madman. . . .
>
> Have you not heard of him at the cross-roads of India? And in the land of the Magi, and upon the sands of Egypt?
>
> And here in your North Country, your bards of old sang of Prometheus the fire-bringer, he who was the desire of human beings fulfilled, the caged hope made free.
>
> And Orpheus, who came with a voice and a lyre to quicken the spirit in beasts and people.

The following year (1913) Gibran also met Swiss psychiatrist C.G. Jung, just as the latter was beginning to formulate his theories of the "collective unconscious," a vast repository of archetypes, images, and stories shared by all humanity in a common storehouse of consciousness. Gibran expresses this idea in one of his pithy aphorisms from *Sand and Foam* (1926):

> I long for eternity
> because there I shall meet
> my unwritten poems and
> my unpainted pictures.

Some mystics follow a definite spiritual path, and we can label them "Sufis," "Jewish mystics," "Christian mystics," and so forth. They may start their own school or carry on an existing one. Others follow their own unique path, one that no one else can or should follow. Here we might think of contemporaries of Gibran—"natural" American mystics like poets Walt Whitman or Edna St. Vincent Millay.

One of Gibran's biographers, Suheil Bushrui, expresses it this way:

> Was Gibran a Christian? There is no doubt that he had accepted the Christian revelation, taking Jesus as an exemplar and the Bible as a treasury of revealed spiritual and moral truth. However, true to the followers of the Sufi path, he could not accept Christianity as exclusive. . . . His creed involved a diversity of strands of belief: the *Upanishads*; Syrian Neoplatonism; Judeo-Christian mysticism; Islamic Sufism; and the Baha'i teachings on universal love and the unity of religion as he heard them from Abdul Baha. . . . He forged his own personal spiritual philosophy in which he would connect all the traditions and join William Blake in declaring that "all religions are one" (Bushrui and Jenkins 1998, p. 266).

On the actual editing of this book: it is clear that Gibran was helped with his grammar and punctuation by various people, particularly his long-time patron, muse and editor Mary Haskell. As the way we read has changed over the past hundred years, so has grammar, so I have re-punctuated or re-lined many selections to seek to bring out the rhythm of Gibran's voice for the modern reader.

As far as Gibran's use of gender-inclusive or exclusive terms go, I have taken a light touch in attempting to preserve his intent, keeping in mind the Arabic language in which he thought. Throughout his writing, Gibran often refers to God as "he," but he also refers to Life as "she," and makes frequent references to "goddesses." In the total picture, things balance out, which is what one finds in reading gendered languages like ancient Hebrew or classical Arabic, where the sun, moon, and various living beings of nature have gendered forms. In one exception to this editing policy, I have substituted "humanity" for "mankind." This does not disturb the rhythm of Gibran's voice, is more faithful to the underlying (and gender neutral) Arabic word he was thinking of, and is a more accurate way of including us all.

In selecting the material for this book, I have placed well-known sayings of Gibran next to lesser-known ones. We begin with Gibran the seeker musing about life's paradoxes and its games of hide-and-seek. Then we proceed to progressively deeper questions: life and death, good and evil, success and failure. Finally, we harvest Gibran's insights on traveling the inner path as he sought to solve these insolvable questions, as well as the ultimate question: who does the traveling, anyway?

Arguably, if one publishes a "book of secrets," the secrets would then cease to be secrets. Point taken. However, we can say that Gibran's deepest-felt words point us towards answers to life's biggest questions, answers that cannot be spoken aloud but only recognized and confirmed in our own unique life experiences.

Neil Douglas-Klotz
Fife, Scotland
February 2018

NOTES

Bushrui, S. and J. Jenkins. (1998). *Kahlil Gibran: Man and Poet*. Oxford: Oneworld.

Douglas-Klotz, Neil (2011). *Desert Wisdom: A Nomad's Guide to Life's Big Questions from the Heart of the Native Middle East*. Columbus, OH: ARC Books.

Martin, Nicholas, editor. (2015). *The Arabic Plays of Kahlil Gibran*. Plano, TX: Martin. Excerpts reprinted with permission. All rights reserved.

Kahlil Gibran's

LITTLE BOOK OF SECRETS

1

Entering the Labyrinth of Life

The riddles of life both bedevil and amuse us. Without these puzzles, these games of hide and seek, would we find any interest in life, any reason to continue moving ahead towards life's purpose?

Like Ink and Paper

Some of us are like ink and some like paper.

If it were not for the blackness of some of us,
 some of us would be dumb.

And if it were not for the whiteness of some
 of us,
 some of us would be blind.

A Sheet of Snow-White Paper

Said a sheet of snow-white paper:

"Pure was I created, and pure will I remain forever. I would rather be burnt and turn to white ashes than suffer darkness to touch me or the unclean to come near me."

The ink bottle heard what the paper was saying, and it laughed in its dark heart. But it never dared to approach her. And the multi-colored pencils heard her also, and they too never came near her.

And the snow-white sheet of paper did remain pure and chaste forever.

Pure and chaste—and empty.

ANGELS AND DEVILS

If you do not see
the angels and devils
in the beauty and malice of life,
you will be far removed from knowledge,
and your spirit will
be empty of affection.

Inefficiency

Said a hunted fox followed by twenty horsemen and a pack of twenty hounds:

"Of course they will kill me. But how poor and how stupid they must be. Surely it would not be worthwhile for twenty foxes riding on twenty asses and accompanied by twenty wolves to chase and kill one man!"

Worms Turn

Worms will turn.

But is it not strange that
even elephants will yield?

THE RELATIVE VALUE OF SPEED

Said a skunk to a tuberose,
"See how swiftly I run, while you cannot walk
    or even creep."
Said the tuberose to the skunk,
"Oh, most noble swift runner, please run
    swiftly!"

Turtles can tell more about roads than hares.

SPACE

Space is not space
between the earth and the sun
to one who looks down
from the windows of the Milky Way.

How I Became a Madman

You ask me how I became a madman. It happened thus:

One day, long before many gods were born, I woke from a deep sleep and found all my masks were stolen—the seven masks I had fashioned and worn in seven lives.

I ran maskless through the crowded streets shouting, "Thieves, thieves, the cursed thieves!"

Men and women laughed at me, and some ran to their houses in fear of me.

And when I reached the marketplace, a youth standing on a housetop cried, "He is a madman!"

I looked up to behold him. For the first time, the sun kissed my own naked face, and my soul was inflamed with love for the sun. I wanted my masks no more. As if in a trance I cried, "Blessed, blessed are the thieves who stole my masks!"

Thus I became a madman.

And I have found both the freedom of loneliness and the safety from being understood, for those who understand us enslave something in us.

But let me not be too proud of my safety.

Even a thief in a jail is safe from another thief.

VEILS

The mountain veiled in mist is not a hill.

An oak tree in the rain is not a weeping willow.

MASKS OF LIFE

Even the masks of life
are masks of deeper mystery.

FACES

I have seen a face with a thousand countenances, and a face that was but a single countenance, as if held in a mold.

I have seen a face whose sheen I could look through to the ugliness beneath and a face whose sheen I had to lift to see how beautiful it was.

I have seen an old face much lined with nothing and a smooth face in which all things were graven.

I know faces, because I look through the fabric that my own eye weaves and behold the reality beneath.

UGLINESS

Is it not that which you have never striven to reach, into whose heart you have never desired to enter, that you deem ugliness?

If ugliness is anything, indeed it is but the scales upon our eyes and the wax filling our ears.

Call nothing ugly, my friend, save the fear of a soul in the presence of its own memories.

THE SCARECROW

Once I said to a scarecrow, "You must be tired of standing in this lonely field."

And he said, "The joy of scaring is a deep and lasting one, and I never tire of it."

Said I, after a minute of thought, "It is true, for I too have known that joy."

Said he, "Only those who are stuffed with straw can know it."

Then I left him, not knowing whether he had complimented or belittled me.

A year passed, during which time the scarecrow turned philosopher. And when I passed by him again I saw two crows building a nest under his hat.

Spring and Winter

The flowers of spring
are winter's dreams
related at the breakfast table
of the angels.

A Meeting Time

We measure time
according to the movement
of countless suns.

They measure time
by little machines
in their little pockets.

Now tell me,
how could we ever meet
at the same place
and the same time?

·Remembrance and Forgetfulness

Remembrance is a form of meeting.

Forgetfulness is a form of freedom.

The Wise King

Once in the distant city of Wirani a king ruled who was both mighty and wise. And he was feared for his might and loved for his wisdom.

Now, in the heart of that city was a well whose water was cool and crystalline, from which all the inhabitants drank, even the king and his courtiers, for there was no other well.

One night when all were asleep, a witch entered the city and poured seven drops of strange liquid into the well. She said, "From this hour whoever drinks this water shall become mad."

The next morning all the inhabitants, save the king and his lord chamberlain, drank from the well and became mad, even as the witch had foretold.

And during that day the people in the narrow streets and in the marketplaces did nothing but whisper to one another, "The king is mad. Our king and his lord chamberlain have lost their reason. Surely we cannot be ruled by a mad king. We must dethrone him."

That evening the king ordered a golden goblet to be filled from the well. And when it was brought to him, he drank deeply and gave it to his lord chamberlain to drink.

And there was great rejoicing in that distant city of Wirani, because its king and its lord chamberlain had regained their reason.

WHITE DOVES

Seven centuries ago, seven white doves rose from a deep valley, flying to the snow-white summit of the mountain.

One of the seven men who watched the flight said, "I see a black spot on the wing of the seventh dove."

Today the people in that valley tell of seven black doves who flew to the summit of the snowy mountain.

HISTORY

Upon the road of Zaad, a traveler met a man who lived in a nearby village.

And the traveler, pointing to a vast field, asked the man, "Was not this the battleground where King Ahlam overcame his enemies?"

And the man answered, "This has never been a battleground. There once stood on this field the great city of Zaad, and it was burnt down to ashes. But now it is a good field, is it not?"

And the traveler and the man parted.

Not a half mile farther, the traveler met another man and pointing to the field again said, "So that is where the great city of Zaad once stood?"

And the man said, "There has never been a city in this place. But once there was a monastery here, and it was destroyed by the people of the South Country."

Shortly after on that very road of Zaad, the traveler met a third man and, pointing once more to the same vast field, he said, "Is it not true that this is the place where once there stood a great monastery?"

But the man answered, "There has never been a monastery in this neighborhood, but our fathers and our forefathers have told us that once there fell a great meteor on this field."

Then the traveler walked on, wondering in his heart. And he met a very old man, and saluting him he said, "Sir, upon this road I have met three men who live in the neighborhood, and I have asked each of them about this field, and each one denied what the other had said, and each one told me a new tale that the other had not told."

Then the old man raised his head and answered, "My friend, each and every one of these men told you what was indeed so.

"But few of us are able to add one fact to a different fact and make a truth out of them."

Full and Empty

Had I filled myself with all that you know,
what room should I have
for all that you do not know?

I have learned silence from the talkative,
toleration from the intolerant,
and kindness from the unkind.

Yet it's strange:
I am ungrateful to these teachers.

EMPTY CUP

When my cup is empty,
I resign myself to its emptiness.
But when it is half full,
I resent its half-fulness.

A Hand Filled with Mist

Once I filled my hand with mist.
Then I opened it and lo,
the mist was a worm.

And I closed and opened my hand again,
and behold, there was a bird.

And again I closed and opened my hand,
and in its hollow stood a man
with a sad face turned upward.

And again I closed my hand,
and when I opened it
there was naught but mist.

But I heard a song of exceeding sweetness.

City of the Heart's Desire

Once there came from the desert to the great city of Sharia a man who was a dreamer, and he had naught but his garment and staff.

And as he walked through the streets, he gazed with awe and wonder at the temples and towers and palaces, for the city of Sharia was of surpassing beauty. And he spoke often to the passersby, questioning them about their city. But they understood not his language, nor he their language.

At the noon hour, he stopped before a vast inn. It was built of yellow marble, and people were going in and coming out unhindered.

"This must be a shrine," he said to himself, and he too went in. But what was his surprise to find himself in a hall of great splendor and a large company of men and women seated about many tables. They were eating and drinking and listening to the musicians.

"Nay," said the dreamer. "This is no worshipping. It must be a feast given by the prince to the people in celebration of a great event."

At that moment a man, whom he took to be the slave of the prince, approached him and bade him be seated. And he was served with meat and wine and most excellent sweets.

When he was satisfied, the dreamer rose to depart. At the door he was stopped by a large man magnificently arrayed.

"Surely this is the prince himself!" said the dreamer in his heart, and he bowed to him and thanked him.

Then the large man said in the language of the city:

"Sir, you have not paid for your dinner." And the dreamer did not understand and again thanked him heartily. Then the large man bethought him, and he looked more closely upon the dreamer. And he saw that he was a stranger, clad in but a poor garment, and that indeed he had not wherewith to pay for his meal.

Then the large man clapped his hands and called, and there came four watchmen of the city.

And they listened to the large man. Then they took the dreamer between them, and they were two on each side of him.

And the dreamer noted the ceremoniousness of their dress and of their manner and he looked upon them with delight. "These," said he, "are men of distinction!"

And they walked all together until they came to the House of Judgment, and they entered.

The dreamer saw before him, seated upon a throne, a venerable man with flowing beard, robed majestically. And he thought he was the king. And he rejoiced to be brought before him.

Now the watchmen related to the judge, who was the venerable man, the charge against the dreamer, and the judge appointed two advocates, one to present the charge and the other to defend the stranger. And the advocates rose, the one after the other, and delivered each his argument. And the dreamer thought himself to be listening to addresses of welcome, and his heart filled with gratitude to the king and the prince for all that was done for him.

Then sentence was passed upon the dreamer, that upon a tablet about his neck his crime should be written, and that he should ride through the city on a naked horse, with a trumpeter and a drummer before him. And the sentence was carried out forthwith.

Now as the dreamer rode through the city upon the naked horse, with the trumpeter and the drummer before him, the inhabitants of the city came running forth at the sound of the noise, and when they saw him they laughed one and all, and the children ran after him in companies, from street to street.

And the dreamer's heart was filled with ecstasy, and his eyes shone upon them. For to him the tablet was a sign of the king's blessing and the procession was in his honor.

Now as he rode, he saw among the crowd a man who was from the desert like himself, and his heart swelled with joy. And he cried out to him with a shout:

"Friend! Friend! Where are we? What city of the heart's desire is this? What race of lavish hosts, who feast the chance guest in their palaces, whose princes companion him, whose king hangs a token upon his breast and opens to him the hospitality of a city descended from heaven!"

And he who was also of the desert replied not. He only smiled and slightly shook his head. And the procession passed on.

And the dreamer's face was uplifted, and his eyes were overflowing with light.

THE BLESSED CITY

In my youth I was told that in a certain city everyone lived according to the Scriptures.

And I said, "I will seek that city and the blessedness thereof." And it was far. I made great provision for my journey. And after forty days I beheld the city, and on the forty-first day I entered into it.

And lo! The whole company of the inhabitants had each but a single eye and but one hand. And I was astonished and said to myself, "Shall they of this so holy city have but one eye and one hand?"

Then I saw that they too were astonished, for they were marvelling greatly at my two hands and my two eyes. And as they were speaking together, I inquired of them saying, "Is this indeed the Blessed City, where each man lives according to the Scriptures?" And they said, "Yes, this is that city."

"And what," said I, "hath befallen you, and where are your right eyes and your right hands?"

And all the people were moved. And they said, "Come thou and see."

And they took me to the temple in the midst of the city. And in the temple I saw a heap of hands and eyes, all withered. Then said I, "Alas! what conqueror hath committed this cruelty upon you?"

And there went a murmur amongst them. And one of their elders stood forth and said, "This doing is of ourselves. God hath made us conquerors over the evil that was in us."

And he led me to a high altar, and all the people followed. And he showed me above the altar an inscription graven, and I read:

"If thy right eye offend thee, pluck it out and cast it from thee. For it is profitable for thee that one of thy members should perish, and not that thy whole body should be cast into hell. And if thy right hand offend thee, cut if off and cast it from thee. For it is profitable for thee that one of thy members should perish, and not that thy whole body should be cast into hell."

Then I understood. And I turned about to all the people and cried, "Hath no man or woman among you two eyes or two hands?"

And they answered me saying, "No, not one. There is none whole save such as are yet too young to read the Scripture and to understand its commandment."

And when we had come out of the temple, I straightway left that Blessed City. For I was not too young, and I could read the Scripture.

A Rock and a Riddle

And on the first day of the week when the sounds of the temple bells sought their ears, one spoke and said, "Master, we hear much talk of God hereabout. What say you of God, and who is God in very truth?"

And he stood before them like a young tree, fearless of wind or tempest, and he answered saying:

Think now, my comrades and beloved, of a heart that contains all your hearts, a love that encompasses all your loves, a spirit that envelops all your spirits, a voice enfolding all your voices, and a silence deeper than all your silences, and timeless.

Seek now to perceive in your self-fulness a beauty more enchanting than all things beautiful, a song more vast than the songs of the sea and the forest, a majesty seated upon the throne for which Orion is but a footstool, holding a sceptre in which the Pleiades are naught save the glimmer of dewdrops.

You have sought always only food and shelter, a garment and a staff. Seek now one who is neither an aim for your arrows nor a stony cave to shield you from the elements.

And if my words are a rock and a riddle, then seek nonetheless, that your hearts may be broken and that your questionings may bring you unto the love and the wisdom of the Most High, whom people call God.

2

Secrets of Life and Death

Life and death may be the ultimate questions
of existence, yet they seem to be the ones that
we spend most of our lives avoiding. Can the
awareness that these bodies don't last forever
cause us to put the present moment
to better use?

Death Is Not Nearer

Death is not nearer
to the aged
than to the newborn.
Neither is life.

FUNERALS

Maybe a funeral among human beings
is a wedding feast among the angels.

A forgotten reality may die
and leave in its will
seven thousand actualities and facts
to be spent on its funeral
and the building of a tomb.

The City of the Dead

Yesterday I drew myself from the noisy throngs and proceeded into the field until I reached a knoll upon which nature had spread her comely garments. Now I could breathe.

I looked back, and the city appeared with its magnificent mosques and stately residences, veiled by the smoke of the shops.

I commenced analyzing humanity's mission, but could conclude only that most of its life was identified with struggle and hardship. Then I tried not to ponder what the sons of Adam had done and centered my eyes on the field that is the throne of God's glory. In one secluded corner of the field I observed a burying ground surrounded by poplar trees.

There, between the city of the dead and the city of the living, I meditated. I thought of the eternal silence in the first and the endless sorrow in the second.

In the city of the living I found hope and despair, love and hatred, joy and sorrow, wealth and poverty, faith and infidelity.

In the city of the dead there is buried earth in earth, which nature converts in the night's silence into vegetation and then into animal and then into human being.

As my mind wandered in this fashion, I saw a procession moving slowly and reverently, accompanied by pieces of music that filled the sky with sad melody. It was an elaborate funeral. The dead was followed by the living, who wept and lamented his going. As the cortege reached the place of interment, the priests commenced praying and burning incense and the musicians blowing and plucking their instruments, mourning the departed. Then the leaders came forward, one after the other, and recited their eulogies with fine choices of words.

At last the multitude departed, leaving the dead resting in a most spacious and beautiful vault, expertly designed in stone and iron and surrounded by the most expensively entwined wreaths of flowers.

The farewell-bidders returned to the city, and I remained, watching them from a distance and speaking softly to myself. Meanwhile the sun was descending to the horizon, and nature was making her many preparations for slumber.

Then I saw two men laboring under the weight of a wooden casket, and behind them a shabby-appearing woman carrying an infant in her arms. Following last was a dog which, with heartbreaking eyes, stared first at the woman and then at the casket.

It was a poor funeral. This guest of death left to cold society a miserable wife and an infant to share her sorrows and a faithful dog whose heart knew of his companion's departure.

As they reached the burial place, they deposited the casket into a ditch away from the tended shrubs and marble stones, and retreated after a few simple words to God. The dog made one last turn to look at his friend's grave as the small group disappeared behind the trees.

I looked at the city of the living and said to myself, "That place belongs to the few." Then I looked upon the grim city of the dead and said,

"That place, too, belongs to the few. O Lord, where is the haven of all the people?"

As I said this, I looked toward the clouds mingled with the sun's longest and most beautiful golden rays.

And I heard a voice within me saying:

"Over there!"

No Graves Here

And behold,
I have found that which is
greater than wisdom.

It is a flame spirit in you,
ever gathering more of itself,
while you, heedless of its expansion,
bewail the withering of your days.

It is life in quest of life,
in bodies that fear the grave.

There are no graves here.
These mountains and plains are
a cradle and a stepping-stone.

Whenever you pass by the field
where you have laid your ancestors,
look well thereupon, and you shall see
yourselves and your children
dancing hand-in-hand.

Only a Difference in Heartbeats

And one day, as Phardrous the Greek walked in the garden, he struck his foot upon a stone, and he was angered. And he turned and picked up the stone, saying in a low voice, "O dead thing in my path!" and he flung away the stone.

And Almustafa, the chosen and the beloved said, "Why say you, 'O dead thing?' Have you been so long in this garden and know not that there is nothing dead here? All things live and glow in the knowledge of the day and the majesty of the night. You and the stone are one. There is a difference only in heartbeats. Your heart beats a little faster, does it, my friend? Aye, but it is not so tranquil.

"Its rhythm may be another rhythm, but I say unto you that if you sound the depths of your soul and scale the heights of space, you shall hear one melody.

"And in that melody the stone and the star sing, the one with the other, in perfect unison."

DEATH IS THE REVEALER

The tax collector Zacchaeus[1] speaks of the fate of Jesus:

You believe what you hear said. Believe in the unsaid, for the silence of people is nearer the truth than their words.

You ask if Jesus could have escaped his shameful death and saved his followers from persecution.

He knew his fate and the morrow of his constant lovers. He foretold and prophesied what should befall every one of us. He sought not his death, but he accepted death just as a farmer shrouding his corn with earth accepts the winter and then awaits the spring and harvest. And as a builder lays the largest stone in the foundation.

---

1. According to the story in Luke 18, Zacchaeus climbed a tree to view Jesus as the latter passed through Jericho. Jesus shocked the crowd by stopping under the tree and telling Zacchaeus that he would visit the tax collector's home.

We were men of Galilee and from the slopes of Lebanon. Our master could have led us back to our country to live with his youth in our gardens until old age should come and whisper us back into the years.

He could have done this had he so chosen.

But he knew that to build the temple invisible he must needs lay himself as the cornerstone and lay us around as little pebbles cemented close to himself.

He knew that the sap of his tree must rise from its roots, and he poured his blood upon its roots. And to him it was not sacrifice but rather gain.

Death is the revealer. The death of Jesus revealed his life.

Had he escaped you and his enemies, you would have been the conquerors of the world. Therefore he did not escape.

Only he who desires all shall give all.

Aye, Jesus could have escaped his enemies and lived to old age. But he knew the passing of the seasons, and he would sing his song.

What man, facing the armed world, would not be conquered for the moment so that he might overcome the ages?

And now you ask who in very truth slew Jesus: the Romans or the priests of Jerusalem?

Neither the Romans slew him, nor the priests.

The whole world stood to honor him upon that hill.

DRINKING FROM THE RIVER OF SILENCE

Your fear of death is but the trembling of the shepherd when he stands before the king, whose hand is to be laid upon him in honor.

Is the shepherd not joyful beneath his trembling, that he shall wear the mark of the king? Yet is he not more mindful of his trembling?

For what is it to die but to stand naked in the wind and to melt into the sun? And what is it to cease breathing but to free the breath from its restless tides, that it may rise and expand and seek God unencumbered?

Only when you drink from the river of silence shall you indeed sing.

And when you have reached the mountaintop, then you shall begin to climb.

And when the earth shall claim your limbs, then shall you truly dance.

EVERY SINGLE SEED

Every single seed
that autumn drops into the
dust of the soil
has its own special way
of extracting the heart
from the husk
and of creating from it
its leaves,
then flowers,
and then fruits.

Yet however their ways may differ,
the destination of all seeds
will remain but one,
and that destination is to
stand before the face of the sun.

THE DYING MAN AND THE VULTURE

Wait, wait yet awhile, my eager friend.

I shall yield but too soon this wasted thing
whose agony, overwrought and useless,
exhausts your patience.

I would not have your honest hunger
wait upon these moments.
But this chain, though made of breath,
is hard to break.

And the will to die,
stronger than all things strong,
is stayed by a will to live,
feebler than all things feeble.

Forgive me, comrade.
I tarry too long.
It is memory that holds my spirit,
a procession of distant days,
a vision of youth spent in a dream,
a face that bids my eyelids not to sleep,
a voice that lingers in my ears,
a hand that touches my hand.

Forgive me that you have waited too long.
It is over now, and all is faded:
the face, the voice, the hand
and the mist that brought them hither.

The knot is untied.
The cord is cleaved.
And that which is neither
food nor drink is withdrawn.

Approach, my hungry comrade.
The board is made ready.
And the fare, frugal and spare,
is given with love.

Come, and dig your beak here
into the left side
and tear out of its cage
this smaller bird,
whose wings can beat no more.

I would have it soar with you
into the sky.

Come now, my friend.
I am your host tonight
and you my welcome guest.

Two Quests

A thousand years ago, two philosophers met on a slope of Lebanon, and one said to the other, "Where goest thou?"

And the other answered, "I am seeking after the fountain of youth, which I know wells out among these hills. I have found writings that tell of that fountain, flowering toward the sun. And you, what are you seeking?"

The first man answered, "I am seeking after the mystery of death."

Then each of the two philosophers conceived that the other was lacking in his great science, and they began to wrangle and to accuse each other of spiritual blindness.

Now while the two philosophers were loud upon the wind, a stranger, a man who was deemed a simpleton in his own village, passed by. And when he heard the two in hot dispute, he stood awhile and listened to their argument.

Then he came near to them and said, "My good men, it seems that you both really belong to the same school of philosophy and that you are speaking of the same thing, only you speak in different words. One of you seeks the fountain of youth, and the other seeks the mystery of death. Yet indeed they are but one, and as one they dwell in you both."

Then the stranger turned away saying, "Farewell sages." And as he departed, he laughed a patient laughter.

The two philosophers looked at each other in silence for a moment, and then they laughed also.

And one of them said, "Well now, shall we not walk and seek together?"

LONGING FOR ETERNITY

I long for eternity
because there I shall meet
my unwritten poems and
my unpainted pictures.

Towers of Our Bones

Nay, we have not lived in vain.
Have they not built towers of our bones?

The Beauty of Death

Part One—The Calling

Let me sleep,
for my soul is intoxicated with love.
And let me rest,
for my spirit has had its
bounty of days and nights.

Light the candles and
burn the incense around my bed
and scatter leaves of jasmine and roses
over my body.

Embalm my hair with frankincense
and sprinkle my feet with perfume,
and read what the hand of death
has written on my forehead.

Let me rest in the arms of slumber,
for my open eyes are tired.
Let the silver-stringed lyre
quiver and soothe my spirit.

Weave from the harp and lute
a veil around my withering heart.
Sing of the past as you behold
the dawn of hope in my eyes,
for its magic meaning is a soft bed
upon which my heart rests.

Dry your tears, my friends,
and raise your heads as the flowers
raise their crowns to greet the dawn.

Look at the bride of death
standing like a column of light
between my bed and the infinite.
Hold your breath and listen with me
to the beckoning rustle of her white wings.

Come close and bid me farewell.
Touch my eyes with smiling lips.

Let the children grasp my hands
with soft and rosy fingers.
Let the aged place their veined hands
upon my head and bless me.

Let the virgins come close and
see the shadow of God in my eyes and
hear the echo of God's will
racing with my breath.

Part Two—The Ascending

I have passed a mountain peak,
and my soul is soaring in the firmament
of complete and unbound freedom.

I am far, far away, my companions,
and the clouds are hiding
the hills from my eyes.
The valleys are becoming flooded
with an ocean of silence,
and the hands of oblivion are
engulfing the roads and the houses.

The prairies and fields are
disappearing behind a white specter
that looks like the spring cloud,
yellow as the candlelight
and red as the twilight.

The songs of the waves and
the hymns of the streams
are scattered, and
the voices of the throngs
reduced to silence.

And I can hear nothing but
the music of eternity
in exact harmony
with the spirit's desires.

I am cloaked in full whiteness.
I am in comfort.
I am in peace.

PART THREE—THE REMAINS

Unwrap me from this
white linen shroud
and clothe me with
leaves of jasmine and lilies.

Take my body from the
ivory casket and let it rest
upon pillows of orange blossoms.

Lament me not,
but sing songs of youth and joy.
Shed no tears upon me,
but sing of harvest and the winepress.

Utter no sigh of agony,
but draw upon my face with your finger
the symbol of love and joy.

Disturb not the air's tranquility
with chanting and requiems,
but let your hearts sing with me
the song of eternal life.

Mourn me not with apparel of black,
but dress in color and rejoice with me.

Talk not of my departure
with sighs in your hearts.
Close your eyes and you will see me
with you forevermore.

Place me upon clusters of leaves
and carry me upon your friendly shoulders
and walk slowly to the deserted forest.

Take me not to the crowded burying ground,
lest my slumber be disrupted by
the rattling of bones and skulls.

Carry me to the cypress woods
and dig my grave
where violets and poppies
grow not in the other's shadow.

Let my grave be deep
so that the flood will not carry
my bones to the open valley.

Let my grave be wide,
so that the twilight shadows
will come and sit by me.

Take from me all earthly raiment
and place me deep in my Mother Earth.
And place me with care
upon my mother's breast.

Cover me with soft earth,
and let each handful be mixed with
seeds of jasmine, lilies and myrtle.

And when they grow above me,
and thrive on my body's element,
they will breathe the fragrance of
my heart into space
and reveal even to the sun
the secret of my peace
and sail with the breeze
and comfort the wayfarer.

Leave me then, friends—
leave me and depart on mute feet,
as the silence walks in the deserted valley.

Leave me to God and
disperse yourselves slowly,
as the almond and apple blossoms disperse
under the vibration of Nisan's[2] breeze.

Go back to the joy of your dwellings
and you will find there
that which death cannot remove
from you and me.

Leave with peace,
for what you see here is
far away in meaning
from the earthly world.
Leave me.

---

2. Name of the month of spring in the Middle Eastern calendars,
   usually March through April in the western calendar. The name
   is originally Assyrian-Babylonian, meaning "beginning."

From One Eternity to Another

Humanity is a river of light
running from ex-eternity to eternity.[3]

---

3. While the concept of "ex-eternity" does not exist in English,
   the Arabic language has words for the process of arriving into
   life from "before eternity" (*abadiy)* and of leaving the body for
   "after eternity" (*uzaliy)*. Gibran here plays with this ancient
   Middle Eastern idea of the soul journeying from one eternity
   to another.

A CHANGE OF MASKS

I shall live beyond death,
and I shall sing in your ears,
even after the vast sea wave
carries me back
to the vast sea depth.

I shall sit at your table,
though without a body,
and I shall go with you to your fields,
a spirit invisible.
I shall come to you at your fireside,
a guest unseen.

Death changes nothing
but the masks that cover our faces.
The woodsman shall be still a woodsman.
The plower, a plower.

And those who sang their song to the wind
shall sing it also to the moving spheres.

3

Life's Ups and Downs

Sometimes we seem to be on a roller coaster. Life can be mostly easy and occasionally difficult. Or it can be mostly difficult and only occasionally easy. Can we have one extreme without the other? Is there a way to steady the seesaw of life?

When My Sorrow Was Born

When my Sorrow was born, I nursed it with care and watched over it with loving tenderness.

And my Sorrow grew like all living things, strong and beautiful and full of wondrous delights.

And we loved one another, my Sorrow and I, and we loved the world about us. For Sorrow had a kindly heart, and mine was kindly with Sorrow.

And when we conversed, my Sorrow and I, our days were winged and our nights were girdled with dreams. For Sorrow had an eloquent tongue, and mine was eloquent with Sorrow.

And when we sang together, my Sorrow and I, our neighbors sat at their windows and listened. For our songs were deep as the sea, and our melodies were full of strange memories.

And when we walked together, my Sorrow and I, people gazed at us with gentle eyes and whispered in words of exceeding sweetness. And there were those who looked with envy upon us, for Sorrow was a noble thing, and I was proud with Sorrow.

But my Sorrow died, like all living things, and I am left alone to muse and ponder.

And now when I speak, my words fall heavily upon my ears.

And when I sing my songs, my neighbours come not to listen.

And when I walk the streets, no one looks at me.

Only in my sleep I hear voices saying in pity, "See, there lies the man whose Sorrow is dead."

A WALL BETWEEN TWO GARDENS

Sadness is but a wall between two gardens.

We choose our joys and our sorrows
long before we experience them.

When either your joy or your sorrow
   becomes great,
the world becomes small.

And When My Joy Was Born

And when my Joy was born I held it in my arms and stood on the housetop shouting, "Come ye, my neighbors, come and see, for Joy this day is born unto me. Come and behold this gladsome thing that laughs in the sun."

But none of my neighbors came to look upon my Joy, and great was my astonishment.

And every day for seven moons I proclaimed my Joy from the housetop. And yet no one heeded me. And my Joy and I were alone, unsought and unvisited.

Then my Joy grew pale and weary, because no other heart but mine beheld its loveliness, and no other lips kissed its lips.

Then my Joy died of isolation.

And now I only remember my dead Joy in remembering my dead Sorrow.

But memory is an autumn leaf that murmurs in the wind and then is heard no more.

THE CUP FROM THE POTTER'S OVEN

Then a woman said, "Speak to us of joy and sorrow." And he answered:

Your joy is your sorrow unmasked.

And the selfsame well from which laughter rises was oftentimes filled with your tears. And how else can it be?

The deeper that sorrow carves into your being, the more joy you can contain.

Is not the cup that holds your wine the very cup that was burned in the potter's oven?

And is not the lute that soothes your spirit the very wood that was hollowed with knives?

When you are joyous, look deep into your heart, and you shall find it is only that which has given you sorrow that is giving you joy.

When you are sorrowful, look again in your heart, and you shall see that in truth you are weeping for that which has been your delight.

Some of you say, "Joy is greater than sorrow," and others say, "Nay, sorrow is the greater." But I say unto you, they are inseparable.

Together they come, and when one sits alone with you at your board, remember that the other is asleep upon your bed.

Verily, you are suspended like scales between your sorrow and your joy. Only when you are empty are you at standstill and balanced.

When the treasure-keeper lifts you to weigh his gold and his silver, needs must your joy or your sorrow rise or fall.

DEFEAT

Defeat, my Defeat, my solitude and my aloof-
    ness—
you are dearer to me than a thousand triumphs,
and sweeter to my heart than all the world's
    glory.

Defeat, my Defeat, my self-knowledge and my
    defiance—
through you I know that I am yet young and
    swift of foot
and not to be trapped by withering laurels.
And in you I have found aloneness
and the joy of being shunned and scorned.

Defeat, my Defeat, my shining sword and
    shield—
in your eyes I have read that
to be enthroned is to be enslaved and
to be understood is to be leveled down and
to be grasped is but to reach one's fullness
and like a ripe fruit to fall and be consumed.

Defeat, my Defeat, my bold companion—
you shall hear my songs
and my cries and my silences.
And none but you shall speak to me of
the beating of wings and urging of seas
and of mountains that burn in the night.
And you alone shall climb
my steep and rocky soul.

Defeat, my Defeat, my deathless courage—
you and I shall laugh together with the storm.
And together we shall dig graves
for all that dies in us,
and we shall stand in the sun with a will,
and we shall be dangerous.

The Dead in Me Buried Their Dead

The disciple Thomas muses about the nature of doubt:

Doubt is a pain too lonely to know that faith is his twin brother.

Doubt is a foundling, unhappy and astray, and though his own mother who gave him birth should find him and enfold him, he would withdraw in caution and in fear.

For doubt will not know truth until its wounds are healed and restored.

I doubted Jesus until he made himself manifest to me and thrust my own hand into his very wounds.

Then indeed I believed, and after that I was rid of my yesterdays and the yesterdays of my forefathers.

The dead in me buried their dead. And the living shall live for the anointed king, even for him who was the son of man.

Yesterday they told me that I must go and utter his name among the Persians and the Hindus.

I shall go. And from this day to my last day, at dawn and at eventide, I shall see my lord rising in majesty and I shall hear him speak.

ONLY THE FRUITFUL TREE

The disciple Matthew relates a saying he remembers from Jesus' Sermon the Mount:

Only the fruitful tree is shaken or stoned for food.

Be not heedful of the morrow, but rather gaze upon today, for sufficient for today is the miracle thereof.

Be not over-mindful of yourself when you give, but be mindful of the necessity. For every giver himself receives from the Father and that much more abundantly.

And give to each according to the other's need. For the Father gives not salt to the thirsty, nor a stone to the hungry, nor milk to the weaned.

Forever Giving Birth, Forever Burying

Suzannah of Nazareth remembers her neighbor Mary:

At dawn she was still standing among us, like a lone banner in the wilderness wherein there are no hosts.

We wept because we knew the morrow of her son. But she did not weep, for she knew also what would befall him.

Her bones were of bronze and her sinews of the ancient elms, and her eyes were like the sky, wide and daring.

Have you heard a thrush sing while its nest burns in the wind?

Have you seen a woman whose sorrow is too much for tears or a wounded heart that would rise beyond its own pain?

You have not seen such a woman, for you have not stood in the presence of Mary.

And you have not been enfolded by the Mother invisible.

When we reached the hill, he was raised high upon the cross.

And I looked at Mary. And her face was not the face of a woman bereaved.

It was the countenance of the fertile earth, forever giving birth, forever burying her children.

BETWEEN CALL AND CALL

The ancient earth gods talk about the nature of
humanity at the dawn of the earth's existence:

Immortal and mortal,
twin rivers calling to the sea.

There is no emptiness
between call and call,
but only in the ear.

Time makes our listening more certain,
and gives it more desire.
Only doubt in the mortal
hushes the sound.
We have outsoared the doubt.

Humanity is a child of our younger heart,
a god in slow arising.
And between its joy and pain
lies our sleeping
and the dreaming thereof.

THE SMALL AND THE GREAT

There lived among the hills a woman and her son, and he was her firstborn and only child.

And the boy died of a fever while the physician stood by.

The mother was distraught with sorrow, and she cried to the physician and besought him saying, "Tell me, tell me, what was it that made quiet his striving and silent his song?"

And the physician said, "It was the fever."

And the mother asked, "What is the fever?"

And the physician answered, "I cannot explain it. It is a thing infinitely small that visits the body, and we cannot see it with the human eye."

Then the physician left her. And she kept repeating to herself, "Something infinitely small. We cannot see it with our human eye."

And at evening the priest came to console her. And she wept and she cried out saying, "O why have I lost my son, my only son, my firstborn?"

And the priest answered, "My child, it is the will of God."

And the woman said, "What is God and where is God? I would see God that I may tear my bosom before him and pour the blood of my heart at his feet. Tell me where I shall find him!"

And the priest said, "God is infinitely vast. He is not to be seen with our human eye."

Then the woman cried out, "The infinitely small has slain my son through the will of the infinitely great! Then what are we? What are *we*?"

At that moment the woman's mother came into the room with the shroud for the dead boy. She had heard the words of the priest and also her daughter's cry. And she laid down the shroud and took her daughter's hand in her own hand.

And she said, "My daughter, we ourselves are the infinitely small and the infinitely great. And we are the path between the two."

A SAVING SMALLNESS

Every great man I have known
had something small in his makeup.
And it was that small something
that prevented inactivity
or madness
or suicide.

O GOD OF LOST SOULS

God of lost souls, thou who are lost amongst the gods, hear me!

Gentle destiny that watches over us mad, wandering spirits, hear me!

I dwell in the midst of a perfect race—I, the most imperfect.

I, a human chaos, a nebula of confused elements. I move among finished worlds—peoples of complete laws and pure order, whose thoughts are assorted, whose dreams are arranged, and whose visions are enrolled and registered.

Their virtues, O God, are measured. Their sins are weighed, and even the countless things that pass in the dim twilight of neither sin nor virtue are recorded and cataloged.

Here days and night are divided into seasons of conduct and governed by rules of blameless accuracy:

To eat, to drink, to sleep, to cover one's nudity, and then to be weary in due time.

To work, to play, to sing, to dance, and then to lie still when the clock strikes the hour.

To think thus, to feel thus much, and then to cease thinking and feeling when a certain star rises above yonder horizon.

To rob a neighbor with a smile, to bestow gifts with a graceful wave of the hand, to praise prudently, to blame cautiously, to destroy a soul with a word, to burn a body with a breath, and then to wash the hands when the day's work is done.

To love according to an established order, to entertain one's best self in a preconceived manner, to worship the gods becomingly, to intrigue the devils artfully, and then to forget all as though memory were dead.

To desire with a motive, to contemplate with consideration, to be happy sweetly, to suffer nobly, and then to empty the cup so that tomorrow may fill it again.

All these things, O God, are conceived with forethought, born with determination, nursed with exactness, governed by rules, directed by reason, and then slain and buried after a prescribed method. And even their silent graves that lie within the human soul are marked and numbered.

It is a perfect world, a world of consummate excellence, a world of supreme wonders, the ripest fruit in God's garden, the master thought of the universe.

But why should I be here, O God?
I, a green seed of unfulfilled passion,
a mad tempest that seeks
neither East nor West,
a bewildered fragment
from a burnt planet?
Why am I here,
O God of lost souls,
thou who art
lost amongst the gods?

4

Secrets of Good and Evil

Right and wrong, good and evil, justice and injustice—are they all relative or are there essential values built into life? Could we do without human laws? Could we do without our moral indignation? Could we live without a Satan? Could we live with a happy God?

IF ALL THEY SAY . . .

If all they say of good and evil were true,
then my life is but one long crime.

THE NEW PLEASURE

Last night I invented a new pleasure, and as I was giving it the first trial, an angel and a devil came rushing toward my house.

They met at my door and fought with each other over my newly-created pleasure.

The one cried, "It is a sin!"

The other, "It is a virtue!"

THE GOOD GOD AND THE EVIL GOD

The Good God and the Evil God met on the mountaintop.

The Good God said, "Good day to you, brother."

The Evil God made no answer.

And the Good God said, "You are in a bad humor today."

"Yes," said the Evil God, "for lately I have been often mistaken for you, called by your name, and treated as if I were you, and it ill-pleases me.

And the Good God said, "But I too have been mistaken for you and called by your name."

The Evil God walked away, cursing the stupidity of human beings.

GUILTY AND INNOCENT

You may judge others
only according to your knowledge of yourself.
Tell me now, who among us is guilty
and who is un-guilty?

The truly just is the one who feels
half guilty of your misdeeds.

Only an idiot or a genius breaks human laws,
and they are the nearest to the heart of God.

Crime is either another name of need
or an aspect of a disease.

Wandering Upon the Wind

It is when your spirit goes
wandering upon the wind
that you, alone and unguarded,
commit a wrong unto others and
therefore unto yourself.
And for that wrong committed
must you knock and wait a while
unheeded at the gate of the blessed.

Like the ocean is your god-self.
It remains forever undefiled.
And like the ether it lifts but the winged.
Even like the sun is your god-self.
It knows not the ways of the mole
nor seeks it the holes of the serpent.

But your god-self dwells not
alone in your being.
Much in you is still human,
and much in you is not yet human
but a shapeless dwarf that walks
asleep in the mist,
searching for its own awakening.

And if any would punish
in the name of righteousness
and lay the axe unto the evil tree,
let them see to its roots.

And verily you will find the roots
of the good and the bad,
the fruitful and the fruitless,
all entwined together
in the silent heart of the earth.

And you judges who would be just—
what judgment pronounce you
upon the one who,
though honest in the flesh,
yet is a thief in spirit?

What penalty lay you upon the one
who slays in the flesh
yet is himself slain in the spirit?

And how prosecute you the one
who in action is a deceiver and an oppressor,
yet who also is aggrieved and outraged?

And how shall you punish those
whose remorse is already
greater than their misdeeds?
Is not remorse the justice
that is administered by that very law
that you would desire to serve?

Yet you cannot lay
remorse upon the innocent
nor lift it from the heart of the guilty.
Unbidden shall it call in the night,
that people may wake and
gaze upon themselves.

And you who would understand justice,
how shall you, unless you look upon
all deeds in the fullness of light?

Only then shall you know that
the erect and the fallen
are but one person,
standing in twilight between
the night of their dwarf-self and
the day of their god-self.

And that the cornerstone of the temple
is not higher than the lowest stone
in its foundation.

SIN, BACKWARD AND FORWARD

If there is such a thing as sin
some of us commit it backward,
following our ancestors' footsteps.
And some of us commit it forward
by overruling our children.

A Ship Without a Rudder
Might Not Sink

And one of the elders of the city said, "Speak to us of good and evil." And Almustafa answered:

Of the good in you I can speak, but not of the evil.

For what is evil but good tortured by its own hunger and thirst?

Verily, when the good is hungry, it seeks food even in dark caves, and when it thirsts, it drinks even of dead waters.

You are good when you are one with yourself.

Yet when you are not one with yourself, you are not evil.

For a divided house is not a den of thieves. It is only a divided house.

And a ship without rudder may wander aimlessly among perilous isles yet sink not to the bottom.

My Faults and Yours

Please do not whitewash
your inherent faults
with your acquired virtues.

I would have the faults.
They are like mine own.

How often have I attributed to myself
crimes I have never committed
so that the other person may feel
comfortable in my presence?

A Higher Court?

At this time the court adjourned and the emir walked out, accompanied by all his wise men, guarded by the soldiers, while the audience scattered and the place became empty except for the moaning and wailing of the prisoners.

All this happened while I was standing there, like a mirror before passing ghosts.

I was meditating on the laws made by humanity for itself, contemplating what people call "justice," and engrossing myself with deep thoughts of the secrets of life.

I tried to understand the meaning of the universe. I was dumbfounded in finding myself lost like a horizon that disappears beyond the cloud.

As I left the place I said to myself, "The vegetable feeds upon the elements of the earth, the sheep eats the vegetable, the wolf preys upon the sheep, and the bull kills the wolf while the lion devours the bull. Yet death claims the lion.

"Is there any power that will overcome death and make these brutalities an eternal justice? Is there a force that can convert all the ugly things into beautiful objects?

"Is there any might that can clutch with its hands all the elements of life and embrace them with joy, as the sea joyfully engulfs all the brooks into its depths?

"Is there any power that can arrest the murdered and the murderer, the adulteress and the adulterer, the robber and the robbed, and bring them to a court loftier and more supreme than the court of the emir?"

THE OLD SERPENT

You delight in laying down laws,
yet you delight more in breaking them,
like children playing by the ocean
who build sand towers with constancy
and then destroy them with laughter.

But while you build your sand towers,
the ocean brings more sand to the shore,
and when you destroy them,
the ocean laughs with you.
Verily, the ocean always laughs with
    the innocent.

But what of those to whom
life is not an ocean
and human laws are not sand towers,
but to whom life is a rock
and the law a chisel with which
they would carve it in their own likeness?

What of the cripple who hates dancers?
What of the ox who loves its yoke
and deems the elk and deer of the forest
stray and vagrant things?

What of the old serpent
who cannot shed its skin
and calls all others naked and shameless?

DRAGONS

Every dragon gives birth to a St. George who slays it.

THE DYING SATAN

Father Samaan's mission in North Lebanon was to travel from one village to another, preaching and curing the people from the spiritual disease of sin and saving them from the horrible trap of Satan. The Reverend Father waged constant war with Satan. The *fellahin* honored and respected this clergyman and were always anxious to buy his advice or prayers with pieces of gold and silver. And at every harvest they would present him with the finest fruits of their fields.

One evening in autumn, as Father Samaan walked his way towards a solitary village, crossing those valleys and hills, he heard a painful cry emerging from a ditch at the side of the road. He stopped and looked in the direction of the voice and saw an unclothed man lying on the ground. Streams of blood oozed from deep wounds in his head and chest. He was moaning painfully for aid, saying, "Save me, help me! Have mercy on me, I am dying."

Father Samaan came close to the man, knelt, and stared at him. But he saw a strange face with contrasting features. He saw intelligence with slyness, ugliness with beauty, and wickedness with softness. He withdrew to his feet sharply and exclaimed, "Who are you?"

With a fainting voice, the dying man said, "Fear me not, Father, for we have been strong friends for long. Help me to stand and take me to the nearby streamlet and cleanse my wounds with your linens." And the Father inquired, "Tell me who you are, for I do not know you, nor even remember having seen you."

And the man replied with an agonizing voice, "You know my identity! You have seen me one thousand times, and you speak of me each day. I am dearer to you than your own life. I am Satan."

The clergyman retorted, "The hands that offer a daily sacrifice to God shall not touch a body made of the secretion of hell. You must die accursed by the tongues of the ages and the lips of humanity, for you are the enemy of humanity, and it is your avowed purpose to destroy all virtue."

Satan moved in anguish, raising himself upon one elbow and responded, "You know not what you are saying nor understand the crime you are committing upon yourself. Give heed, for I will relate my story.

"Today I walked alone in this solitary valley. When I reached this place, a group of angels descended to attack and struck me severely. Had it not been for one of them who carried a blazing sword with two sharp edges, I would have driven them off, but I had no power against the brilliant sword."

And Satan ceased talking for a moment, as he pressed a shaking hand upon a deep wound in his side. Then he continued, "The armed angel—I believe he was Michael—was an expert gladiator. Had I not thrown myself to the friendly ground and feigned to have been slain, he would have torn me into brutal death."

With voice of triumph, and casting his eyes heavenward, the Father offered, "Blessed be Michael's name, who has saved humanity from this vicious enemy."

And Satan protested, "My disdain for humanity is not greater than your hatred for yourself. You are blessing Michael, who never has come to your rescue. You are cursing me in the hour of my defeat, even though I was, and still am, the source of your tranquility and happiness. You deny me your blessing and extend not your kindness, but you live and prosper in the shadow of my being. You have adopted my existence as an excuse and weapon for your career, and you employ my name in justification for your deeds. Has not my past caused you to be in need of my present and future? Have you reached your goal in amassing the required wealth? Have you found it impossible to extract more gold and silver from your followers using my kingdom as a threat?

"Do you not realize that you will starve to death if I were to die? What would you do tomorrow if you allowed me to die today? What vocation would you pursue if my name disappeared? For decades you have been roaming these villages and warning the people against falling into my hands. They have bought your advice with their poor dinars and with the products of their land. What would they buy from you tomorrow if they discovered that their wicked enemy no longer existed? Your occupation would die with me, for the people would be safe from sin.

"As a clergyman, do you not realize that Satan's existence alone has created his enemy, the church? That ancient conflict is the secret hand that removes the gold and silver from the faithful's pocket and deposits it forever into the pouch of the preacher and the missionary. How can you permit me to die here, when you know it will surely cause you to lose your prestige, your church, your home, and your livelihood?"

Satan became silent for a moment, and his humility was now converted into a confident independence. He continued, "Father, you are proud, but ignorant. I will disclose to you the history of belief, and in it you will find the truth that joins both of our beings and ties my existence with your very conscience.

"In the first hour of the beginning of time, a human being stood before the face of the sun and stretched forth its arms and cried for the first time saying, 'Behind the sky there is a great and loving and benevolent God.' Then it turned its back to the great circle of light and saw its shadow upon the earth and hailed, 'In the depths of the earth there is a dark evil who loves wickedness.'

"And the human being walked towards its cave, whispering to itself, "I am between two compelling forces, one in whom I must take refuge and the other against whom I must struggle.'

"And the ages marched in procession while human beings existed between two powers, one that they blessed because it exalted them, and one that they cursed because it frightened them. But they never perceived the meaning of a blessing or of a curse. They were between the two, like a tree between summer when it blooms and winter when it shivers.

"When someone saw the dawn of civilization, which is human understanding, the family as a unit came into being. Then came the tribes, whereupon labor was divided according to ability and inclination. One clan cultivated the land, another built shelters, others wove raiment or hunted food. Subsequently divination made its appearance upon the earth, and this was the first career adopted by humanity that possessed no essential urge or necessity."

"In Babylon, the people bowed seven times in worshipping before a priest who fought me with his chanting. In Nineveh, they looked upon a man, who claimed to have known my inner secrets, as a golden link between God and humanity. In Tibet, they called the person who wrestled with me the son of the sun and moon. In Byblos, Ephesus, and Antioch, they offered their children's lives in sacrifice to my opponents. In Jerusalem and Rome, they placed their lives in the hands of those who claimed they hated me and fought me with all their might.

"In every city under the sun, my name was the axis of the educational circle of religion, arts, and philosophy. Had it not been for me, no temples would have been built, no towers or palaces would have been erected. I am the courage that creates resolution in human beings. I am the source that provokes originality of thought. I am the hand that moves humanity's hands. I am Satan everlasting. I am Satan, whom people fight in order to keep themselves alive. If they cease struggling against me, slothfulness will deaden their minds and hearts and souls, in accordance with the weird penalties of their tremendous myth.

"I am the enraged and mute tempest that agitates the minds of men and the hearts of women. And in fear of me, they will travel to places of worship to condemn me, or to places of vice to make me happy by surrendering to my will. The monk who prays in the silence of the night to keep me away from his bed is like the prostitute who invites me to her chamber. I am Satan everlasting and eternal.

"I am the builder of convents and monasteries upon the foundation of fear. I build wine shops and wicked houses upon the foundations of lust and self-gratification. If I cease to exist, fear and enjoyment will be abolished from the world, and through their disappearance, desires and hopes will cease to exist in the human heart. Life will become empty and cold, like a harp with broken strings. I am Satan everlasting.

"I am the heart of all evil. Would you wish for human motion to stop through cessation of my heartbeat? Would you accept the result after destroying the cause? I am the cause! Would you allow me to die in this deserted wilderness? Do you desire to sever the bond that exists between you and me? Answer me, clergyman!"

Father Samaan quivered and rubbed his hands nervously, and with apology in his voice he said, "I know now what I had not known an hour ago. Forgive my ignorance. I know that your existence in this world creates temptation, and temptation is a measurement by which God adjudges the value of human souls. It is a scale which Almighty God uses to weigh the spirits. I am certain that if you die, temptation will die, and with its passing, death will destroy the ideal-power, which elevates and alerts people.

"You must live, for if you die and the people know it, their fear of hell will vanish and they will cease worshipping, for naught would be sin. You must live, for in your life is the salvation of humanity from vice and sin. As to myself, I shall sacrifice my hatred for you on the altar of my love for man."

Satan uttered a laugh that rocked the ground and he said, "What an intelligent person you are, Father! And what wonderful knowledge you possess in theological facts! You have found, through the power of your knowledge, a purpose for my existence that I had never understood, and now we realize our need for each other.

"Come close to me, my brother. Darkness is submerging the plains, and half of my blood has escaped upon the sand of this valley, and nothing remains of me but the remnants of a broken body, which death shall soon buy unless you render aid."

Father Samaan rolled up the sleeves of his robe and approached and lifted Satan to his back and walked towards his home.

In the midst of those valleys, engulfed with silence and embellished with the veil of darkness, Father Samaan walked towards the village with his back bent under his heavy burden. His black raiment and long beard were spattered with blood streaming from above him, but he struggled forward, his lips moving in fervent prayer for the life of the dying Satan.

THE DEVIL DIED

The devil died the very day you were born.
Now you do not have to go through hell
to meet an angel.

What Is Law?

Who are those who hanged the thief in the tree? Are they angels descended from heaven or people looting and usurping? Who cut off the murderer's head? Are they divine prophets or soldiers shedding blood wherever they go? Who stoned that adulteress? Were they virtuous hermits who came from their monasteries or humans who loved to commit atrocities with glee, under the protection of ignorant law?

What is law? Who saw it coming with the sun from the depths of heaven? What human being saw the heart of God and found its will or purpose?

In what century did the angels walk among the people and preach to them saying, "Forbid the weak from enjoying life and kill the outlaws with the sharp edge of the sword and step upon the sinners with iron feet?"

Laughing between the Sand and the Wind

The disciple Luke remembers Jesus talking about hypocrites:

Often I have pondered on the heart that shelters all who come from the wasteland to its sanctuary, yet against the hypocrite is closed and sealed.

One day as we rested with him in the garden of pomegranates, I said to him, "Master, you forgive and console the sinner and all the weak and the infirm, excepting only the hypocrite alone."

And he said, "You have chosen your words well when you called the sinners weak and infirm. I do forgive them their weakness of body and their infirmity of spirit. For their failings have been laid upon them by their forefathers, or by the greed of their neighbors.

"But I tolerate not the hypocrites, because they themselves lay a yoke upon the guileless and the yielding.

"Weaklings, whom you call sinners, are like the featherless young that fall from the nest. The hypocrites are the vultures waiting upon a rock for the death of the prey.

"Weaklings are those lost in a desert. But the hypocrites are not lost. They know the way, yet they laugh between the sand and the wind.

"For this cause I do not receive them."

Thus our master spoke, and I did not understand. But I understand now.

Could We Live with a Happy God?

A Roman speaks to a Greek at the time of Jesus:

The Hebrews, like their neighbors the Phoenicians and the Arabs, will not suffer their gods to rest for a moment upon the wind.

They are over-thoughtful of their deity and over-observant of one another's prayer and worship and sacrifice.

While we Romans build marble temples to our gods, these people would discuss their god's nature. When we are in ecstasy, we sing and dance around the altars of Jupiter and Juno, of Mars and Venus. But they in their rapture wear sackcloth and cover their heads with ashes and even lament the day that gave them birth.

And Jesus, the man who revealed God as a being of joy—they tortured him and then put him to death.

These people would not be happy with a happy god. They know only the gods of their pain.

Even Jesus' friends and disciples, who knew his mirth and heard his laughter, make an image of his sorrow, and they worship that image.

And in such worship they rise not to their deity. They only bring their deity down to themselves.

I believe, however, that this philosopher Jesus, who was not unlike Socrates, will have power over his race and perhaps over other races.

For we are all creatures of sadness and of small doubts. And when someone says to us, "Let us be joyous with the gods," we cannot but heed that voice. Strange that the pain of this man has been fashioned into a rite!

These people would discover another Adonis, a god slain in the forest, and they would celebrate his slaying. It is a pity they heed not his laughter.

But let us confess, as Roman to Greek, do even we ourselves hear the laughter of Socrates in the streets of Athens? Is it ever in us to forget the cup of hemlock, even while we are at the theatre of Dionysus?

Do not rather our fathers still stop at the street corners to chat of troubles and to have a happy moment remembering the doleful end of all our great men?

5

Traveling the Inner Path

Where am I going in life? How do I discover the secrets of my own life and of my relationships with others? There seems to be an inner way that makes sense of it all, one traveled by the seers and prophets, but it is not easy. There is no fixed map, and the path involves abandoning previous ideas of who we are. Those whom we idealize as sacred or holy want us to walk through them like doors, rather than remain at the threshold worshipping them. The first step is discovering our own desire and then listening within.

DREAMS AND DESIRE

I would be the least among people
with dreams and the desire to fulfill them
rather than the greatest
with no dreams and no desires.

THE ASTRONOMER

In the shadow of the temple, my friend and I saw a blind man sitting alone. And my friend said, "Behold the wisest man of our land."

Then I left my friend and approached the blind man and greeted him. And we conversed.

After a while I said, "Forgive my question, but since when have you been blind?"

"From my birth," he answered.

Said I, "And what path of wisdom do you follow?"

Said he, "I am an astronomer."

Then he placed his hand upon his breast saying, "I watch all these suns and moons and stars."

IN A SINGLE DROP

Everything in existence
resides in your core,
and all of what is in your core
resides in existence.

There is no separation
between the closest of things and the farthest
or between the highest and the lowest
or between the smallest and the largest.

In a single drop of water
are all the secrets of the seas.
In a single atom
are all the elements of the Earth.
In a single motion of thought
are all of the motions and laws of the world.

Prayer of the Seas and the Forests

I cannot teach you how to pray in words. God listens not to your words save when God utters them through your lips.

And I cannot teach you the prayer of the seas and the forests and the mountains. But you who are born of the mountains and the forests and the seas can find their prayer in your heart.

And if you but listen in the stillness of the night, you shall hear them saying in silence:

Our God,
who art our winged self,
it is thy will in us that wills.
It is thy desire in us that desires.
It is thy urge in us that would
turn our nights, which are thine,
into days, which are thine also.

We cannot ask thee for aught,
for thou knowest our needs
before they are born in us.
Thou art our need,
and in giving us more of thyself,
thou givest us all.

FREEST SONG

The freest song comes not
through bars and wires.

And those for whom
worshipping is a window,
to open but also to shut,
have not yet visited
the house of their soul,
whose windows are open
from dawn to dawn.

MIRACLES

There are three miracles of our brother Jesus
not yet recorded in the Book:

The first, that he was a man like you and me.
The second, that he had a sense of humor.
And the third, that he knew he was a conqueror,
though conquered.

MASTER SINGER

Master, master singer,
master of words unspoken—
seven times was I born,
and seven times have I died
since your last hasty visit
and our brief welcome.

And behold I live again,
remembering a day and a night
among the hills,
when your tide lifted us up.

Thereafter many lands
and many seas did I cross,
and wherever I was led
by saddle or sail,
your name was a prayer
or an argument.

People would bless you or curse you—
the curse, a protest against failure,
the blessing, a hymn of the hunter
who comes back from the hills
with provision for his mate.

Your friends are yet with us
for comfort and support,
and your enemies also,
for strength and assurance.

Your mother is with us.
I have beheld the sheen of her face
in the countenance of all mothers.
Her hand rocks cradles with gentleness,
her hand folds shrouds with tenderness.

And Mary Magdalen is yet in our midst,
she who drank the vinegar of life
and then its wine.

And Judas,
the man of pain and small ambitions,
he too walks the earth.
Even now he preys upon himself,
when his hunger finds nothing else,
and seeks his larger self
in self-destruction.

And John,
he whose youth loved beauty,
is here and he sings,
though unheeded.

And Simon Peter the impetuous,
who denied you that
he might live longer for you,
he too sits by our fire.
He may deny you again
ere the dawn of another day,
yet he would be crucified
for your purpose
and deem himself
unworthy of the honor.

And Caiaphas and Annas
still live their day and
judge the guilty and the innocent.
They sleep upon their feathered beds
while the ones whom they have judged
are whipped with rods.

And the woman who was taken in adultery,
she too walks the streets of our cities
and hungers for bread not yet baked.
And she is alone in an empty house.

And Pontius Pilatus is here also.
He stands in awe before you
and still questions you,
but he dares not risk his station
or defy an alien race.
And he is still washing his hands.

Even now Jerusalem
holds the basin
and Rome the ewer.
And betwixt the two,
a thousand, thousand hands
would be washed to whiteness.

The Saint

In my youth, I once visited a saint in his silent grove beyond the hills. As we were conversing upon the nature of virtue, a brigand came limping wearily up the ridge. When he reached the grove, he knelt down before the saint and said, "O saint, I would be comforted! My sins are heavy upon me!"

And the saint replied, "My sins too are heavy upon me."

And the brigand said, "But I am a thief and a plunderer!"

And the saint replied, "I too am a thief and a plunderer."

And the brigand said, "But I am a murderer, and the blood of many men cries in my ears!"

And the saint replied, "I am a murderer, and in my ears cries the blood of many men."

And the brigand said, "I have committed countless crimes!"

And the saint replied, "I too have committed crimes without number."

Then the brigand stood up and gazed at the saint, and there was a strange look in his eyes. And when he left us, he went skipping down the hill.

And I turned to the saint and said, "Wherefore did you accuse yourself of uncommitted crimes? Don't you see that this man went away no longer believing in you?"

And the saint answered, "It is true he no longer believes in me. But he went away much comforted."

At that moment we heard the brigand singing in the distance, and the echo of his song filled the valley with gladness.

BLESSED ARE

The disciple Matthew remembers his version of the Beatitudes from Jesus' Sermon on the Mount:

Blessed are the serene in spirit.

Blessed are they who are not held by possessions, for they shall be free.

Blessed are they who remember their pain, and in their pain await their joy.

Blessed are they who hunger after truth and beauty, for their hunger shall bring bread and their thirst cool water.

Blessed are the kindly, for they shall be consoled by their own kindliness.

Blessed are the pure in heart, for they shall be one with God.

Blessed are the merciful, for mercy shall be in their portion.

Blessed are the peacemakers, for their spirit shall dwell above the battle, and they shall turn the potter's field into a garden.

Blessed are they who are hunted, for they shall be swift of foot and they shall be winged.

Rejoice and be joyful, for you have found the kingdom of heaven within you.

The singers of old were persecuted when they sang of that kingdom. You too shall be persecuted, and therein lies your honor, therein your reward.

This Very Now

And upon a day, as they sat in the long shadows of the white poplars, one spoke saying, "Master, I am afraid of time. It passes over us and robs us of our youth, and what does it give in return?"

And Almustafa answered and said:

Take up now a handful of good earth.

Do you find in it a seed and perhaps a worm?

If your hand were spacious and enduring enough, the seed might become a forest and the worm a flock of angels.

And forget not that the years, which turn seeds to forests and worms to angels, belong to this Now.

All of the years, this very Now.

THE WIDER ROAD

And Mannus, the inquisitive disciple, looked about him, and he saw plants in flower clinging to the sycamore-tree. And he said, "Behold the parasites, Master. What say you of them? They are thieves with weary eyelids, who steal the light from the steadfast children of the sun, and make fair of the sap that runs into their branches and their leaves."

And Almustafa answered him saying:

My friend, we are all parasites. We who labor to turn the sod into pulsing life are not above those who receive life directly from the sod, without knowing the sod.

Shall a mother say to her child, "I give you back to the forest, which is your greater mother, for you weary me, heart and hand?"

Or shall the singers rebuke their own songs, saying, "Return now to the cave of echoes from whence you came, for your voice consumes my breath?"

And shall the shepherds say to their year-lings, "I have no pasture whereunto I may lead you. Therefore be cut off and become a sacrifice for this cause?"

Nay, my friend. All these things are answered even before they are asked and, like your dreams, are fulfilled before you sleep.

We live upon one another, according to the law ancient and timeless. Let us live thus in loving-kindness. We seek one another in our aloneness, and we walk the road when we have no hearth to sit beside.

My friends and brothers and sisters, the wider road is your fellow human beings.

These plants that live upon the tree draw milk of the earth in the sweet stillness of night, and the earth in her tranquil dreaming sucks at the breast of the sun.

And the sun, even as you and I and all there is, sits in equal honor at the banquet of the Prince, whose door is always open and whose board is always spread.

Mannus, my friend, all there is lives always upon all there is.

And all there is lives in this faith, shoreless upon the bounty of the Most High.

MASTER POET

Master, master poet,
master of words sung and spoken—
they have built temples
to house your name.
And upon every height
they have raised your cross,
a sign and a symbol to
guide their wayward feet.

But not unto your joy.
Your joy is a hill beyond their vision,
and it does not comfort them.

They would honor the man
unknown to them.

What consolation is there in a man
like themselves,
a man whose kindliness is
like their own kindliness,
a god whose love is

like their own love,
and whose mercy is
in their own mercy?

They honor not the man, the living man,
the first man who opened his eyes
and gazed at the sun
with eyelids unquivering.

Nay, they do not know him,
and they would not be like him.

They would be unknown,
walking in the procession
of the unknown.

They would bear sorrow, their sorrow,
and they would not find comfort in your joy.

Their aching heart seeks not consolation
in your words and the song thereof.
And their pain, silent and unshapen,
makes them creatures lonely and unvisited.

Though hemmed about by kin and kind,
they live in fear, un-comraded.

Yet they would not be alone.
They would bend eastward
when the west wind blows.

They call you king,
and they would be in your court.
They pronounce you the messiah,
and they would themselves be
anointed with the holy oil.
Yea, they would live upon your life.

Master, master singer—
your tears were like the showers of May
and your laughter like
the waves of the white sea.

When you spoke,
your words were
the far-off whisper of their lips,
when those lips should be
kindled with fire.

You laughed for the
marrow in their bones
that was not yet ready for laughter.
And you wept for their eyes
that yet were dry.

Your voice fathered their thoughts
and their understanding.
Your voice mothered their words
and their breath.

Seven times was I born
and seven times have I died.
And now I live again,
and I behold you,
the fighter among fighters,
the poet of poets,
king above all kings,
a man half-naked
with your road-fellows.

Every day the bishop
bends down his head
when he pronounces your name.
And every day the beggars say,
"For Jesus' sake,
give us a penny to buy bread!"

We call upon each other,
but in truth we call upon you,
like the floodtide in the spring
of our want and desire,
and when our autumn comes,
like the ebb tide.

High or low,
your name is upon our lips,
the master of infinite compassion.

When Our Silence Turns to Singing

The disciple John of Zebedee speaks of the different titles that people have given Jesus:

Many times the Christ has come to the world, and he has walked many lands. And always he has been deemed a stranger and a madman.

Yet the sound of his voice never descended to emptiness, for human memory keeps alive that which its mind takes no care to keep.

This is the Christ, the innermost and the height, who walks with all human beings towards eternity.

Have you not heard of him at the crossroads of India? And in the land of the Magi, and upon the sands of Egypt?

And here in your North Country, your bards of old sang of Prometheus the fire-bringer, he who was the desire of human beings fulfilled, the caged hope made free.

And Orpheus, who came with a voice and a lyre to quicken the spirit in beasts and people.

And know you not of Mithra the king, and of Zoroaster the prophet of the Persians, who woke from us from ancient sleep and stood at the bed of our dreaming?

We ourselves become the Anointed when we meet in the temple invisible, once every thousand years. Then comes forth one embodied, and at that one's coming, our silence turns to singing.

Yet our ears turn not always to listening nor our eyes to seeing.

Knocking on the Door

It would be fruitless for the visitor
to knock on the door of the house
if there were no one inside
to hear the knocks
and open the door.

What is a human
but a being
standing between
the infinitude of his interior
and the infinitude
of his surroundings?

Were it not for what we have inside,
we would have nothing outside.

LINES AND CIRCLES

The deep and the high
go to the depth or to the height
in a straight line.

Only the spacious
can move in circles.

WHEN GOD ANSWERS

In the ancient days, when the first quiver of speech came to my lips, I ascended the holy mountain and spoke unto God, saying, "Master, I am thy slave. Thy hidden will is my law and I shall obey thee forevermore."

But God made no answer, and like a mighty tempest passed away.

And after a thousand years, I ascended the holy mountain and again spoke unto God saying, "Creator, I am thy creation. Out of clay hast thou fashioned me, and to thee I owe mine all."

And God made no answer, but like a thousand swift wings passed away.

And after a thousand years, I climbed the holy mountain and spoke unto God again saying, "Father, I am thy son. In pity and love thou hast given me birth, and through love and worship I shall inherit thy kingdom."

And God made no answer, and like the mist that veils the distant hills passed away.

And after a thousand years, I climbed the sacred mountain and again spoke unto God saying, "My God, my aim and my fulfillment. I am thy yesterday and thou are my tomorrow. I am thy root in the earth and thou art my flower in the sky, and together we grow before the face of the sun."

Then God leaned over me, and in my ears whispered words of sweetness. Even as the sea that enfolds a brook that runs down to her, God enfolded me.

And when I descended to the valleys and the plains, God was there also.

DRINK YOURSELVES TO THE DREGS

Joseph of Arimathea speaks about Jesus' deeper aims:

Then came the autumn of his passion.

And he spoke to us of freedom, even as he had spoken in Galilee, in the spring of his song. But now his words sought our deeper understanding.

He spoke of leaves that sing only when blown upon the wind.

And of a human being as a cup filled by the ministering angel of the day to quench the thirst of another angel. Yet, whether that cup is full or empty, it shall stand crystalline upon the table of the Most High.

He said, "You are the cup and you are the wine. Drink yourselves to the dregs. Or else remember me and you shall be quenched."

Oil Burning in the Dark

You are spirits though you move in bodies.
And like oil that burns in the dark,
you are flames, though held in lamps.

All that is deathless in you is
free unto the day and the night
and cannot be housed or fettered.
For this is the will of the Most High.

You are God's breath even as the wind
that shall be neither caught nor caged.

Only for Ecstasy and
Sweet Communion

You pray in your distress and in your need. Would that you might pray also in the fullness of your joy and in your days of abundance.

For what is prayer but the expansion of yourself into the living ether?

And if it is for your comfort to pour your darkness into space, it is also for your delight to pour forth the dawning of your heart.

And if you cannot but weep when your soul summons you to prayer, she should spur you again and yet again, though weeping, until you shall come laughing.

When you pray, you rise to meet in the air those who are praying at that very hour and whom, except in prayer, you may not meet.

Therefore let your visit to that temple invisible be for naught but ecstasy and sweet communion.

For if you should enter the temple for no other purpose than asking, you shall not receive.

And if you should enter into it to humble yourself, you shall not be lifted.

Or even if you should enter into it to beg for the good of others, you shall not be heard.

It is enough that you enter the temple invisible.

Master of Our Lonely Hours

Master, master of our lonely hours—
here and there,
between the cradle and the coffin,
I meet your silent brothers and sisters:
those free, unshackled
sons and daughters of
your mother earth and space.

They are like the birds of the sky
and like the lilies of the field.
They live your life, think your thoughts,
and echo your song.

But they are empty-handed,
and they are not crucified
with the great crucifixion,
and therein is their pain.

The world crucifies them every day,
but only in little ways.
The sky is not shaken,
and the earth travails not with her dead.

They are crucified and
there is none to witness their agony.
They turn their faces right and left
and find no one to promise them
a station in his kingdom.

Yet they would be crucified
again and yet again
that your God may be their God,
and your Father their Father.

Master, master lover—
the princess awaits your coming
in her fragrant chamber,
and the married unmarried woman
in her cage.
The harlot who seeks bread
in the streets of her shame,
and the nun in her cloister
who has no husband.
The childless woman, too,
at her window, where frost designs
the forest on the pane—
she finds you in that symmetry,
and she would mother you
and be comforted.

Master, master poet,
master of our silent desires—
the heart of the world quivers
with the throbbing of your heart,
but it burns not with your song.

The world sits
listening to your voice
in tranquil delight,
but it rises not from its seat
to scale the ridges of your hills.

People would dream your dream,
but they would not wake to your dawn,
which is their greater dream.

They would see with your vision,
but they would not drag
their heavy feet to your throne.

Yet many have been
enthroned in your name
and mitered with your power
and have turned your golden visit
into crowns for their heads
and scepters for their hands.

Master, master of light,
whose eye dwells in the
seeking fingers of the blind—
you are still despised and mocked,
a man too weak and infirm to be God,
a God too human to call forth adoration.

Their mass and their hymn,
their sacrament and their rosary,
are for their imprisoned self.
You are their yet-distant self,
their far-off cry,
and their passion.

But master, sky-heart,
knight of our fairer dream—
you do still tread this day.

Neither bows nor spears
shall stay your steps.
You walk through all our arrows.
You smile down upon us,
and though you are
the youngest of us all,
you father us all.

Poet, singer, great heart—
may our God bless your name
and the womb that held you
and the breasts that gave you milk.

And may God forgive us all.

Upon the Sand

Said one man to another, "At the high tide of the sea long ago, with the point of my staff I wrote a line upon the sand. And the people still pause to read it, and they are careful that nothing shall erase it."

And the other man said, "And I too wrote a line upon the sand, but it was at low tide, and the waves of the vast sea washed it away. But tell me, what did you write?"

And the first man answered, "I wrote this: 'I am he who is.' But what did you write?"

And the other man said, "This I wrote: 'I am but a drop of this great ocean.'"

A Seeker of Silences Am I

And as he walked, Almustafa saw from afar men and women leaving their fields and their vineyards and hastening towards the city gates.

And he heard their voices calling his name and shouting from field to field, telling one another of the coming of his ship. And he said to himself:

Shall the day of parting be the day of gathering? And shall it be said that my evening was in truth my dawn?

And what shall I give to those who have left their ploughs in mid-furrow or to the ones who have stopped the wheel of their winepresses?

Shall my heart become a tree, heavy-laden with fruit, which I may gather and give unto them?

And shall my desires flow like a fountain that I may fill their cups?

Am I a harp that the hand of the mighty may touch me, or a flute that their breath may pass through me?

A seeker of silences am I. And what treasure have I found in silences that I may dispense with confidence?

If this is my day of harvest, in what fields have I sowed the seed and in what unremembered seasons?

If this indeed be the hour in which I lift up my lantern, it is not my flame that shall burn therein.

Empty and dark shall I raise my lantern, and the guardian of the night shall fill it with oil and shall light it also.

Sources of the Selections

Spirits Rebellious (1908) SR
The Broken Wings (1912) BW
A Tear and a Smile (1914) TS
The Procession (1918) TP
The Madman (1918) M
The Forerunner (1920) F
The Tempests (1920) T
The Prophet (1923) P
Iram of the Pillars (1923, Arabic edition, see
    below.) IP
Sand and Foam (1926) SF
Jesus The Son of Man (1928) JSM
The Earth Gods (1931) EG

The Wanderer (1932) W
The Garden of the Prophet (1933) GP
Lazarus and His Beloved (1933) LB

Grateful acknowledgement is made to Nicholas Martin for permission to reprint excerpts from Gibran's play "Iram of the Pillars" as translated in *The Arabic Plays of Kahlil Gibran*, Nicholas Martin, editor. Copyright Nicholas R.M. Martin 2015, reprinted with permission, all rights reserved.

ENTERING THE LABYRINTH OF LIFE

Like Ink and Paper (SF)
A Sheet of Snow-White Paper (F)
Angels and Devils (BW)
Inefficiency (SF)
Worms Turn (SF)
The Relative Value of Speed (SF)
Space (SF)
How I Became a Madman (M)
Veils (SF)
Masks of Life (SF)

SECRETS OF LIFE AND DEATH

LIFE'S UPS AND DOWNS

Forever Giving Birth, Forever Burying (JSM)
   "Suzannah of Nazareth, a Neighbor
   of Mary"
Between Call and Call (EG)
The Small and the Great (W)
A Saving Smallness (SF)
O God of Lost Souls (M) "The Perfect World"

SECRETS OF GOOD AND EVIL

If All They Say . . . (SF)
The New Pleasure (M)
The Good God and the Evil God (M)
Guilty and Innocent (SF)
Wandering Upon the Wind (P)
Sin, Backward and Forward (SF)
A Ship Without a Rudder Might Not Sink (P)
My Faults and Yours (SF)
A Higher Court? (SR)
The Old Serpent (P)
Dragons (SF)
The Dying Satan (T)
The Devil Died (SF)
What Is Law? (SR) "The Cry of the Graves"

TRAVELING THE INNER PATH

Knocking on the Door (IP)

Lines and Circles (SF)

When God Answers (M)

Drink Yourselves to the Dregs (JSM) "Joseph of
    Arimathea: On the Primal Aims of Jesus"

Oil Burning in the Dark (GP)

Only for Ecstasy and Sweet Communion (P)

Master of Our Lonely Hours (JSM) "A Man from
    Lebanon Nineteen Centuries Later"

Upon the Sand (W)

A Seeker of Silences Am I (P)

About the Author

Dates from the life of Gibran Khalil Gibran, the author's full Arabic name, which due to a registration spelling mistake at his first school in the United States was changed from the usual spelling to "Kahlil."

1883: Born in Bsharri, a village in the north of Lebanon.

1895: Gibran's mother immigrates to Boston with her four children, hoping to flee poverty and unhappiness, while her husband remains in Lebanon, imprisoned for embezzling from the government.

1898:   Returns to Lebanon to study Arabic
           and French at a Maronite-run pre-
           paratory school in Beirut. By some
           accounts, his mother wants to remove
           him from unsavory artistic influences
           in Boston.

1902:   Returns to Boston. In fifteen months'
           time, he loses his mother, sister, and
           half-brother to tuberculosis.

1904:   Through photographer Fred Holland
           Day he meets Mary Haskell, a school
           headmistress who becomes his
           patron, muse, editor, and possible
           lover. Publishes several poems in
           prose gathered later under the title *A
           Tear and a Smile*.

1908-10:   Funded by Mary, he attends art school
           in Paris.

1911:   Settles in New York where he starts
           an intimate correspondence with May
           Ziadeh, a Lebanese intellectual living
           in Cairo.

1918:   *The Madman*, Gibran's first book written in English, is published.

1920:   Together with other Arab and Lebanese writers and poets living in the United States, he founds a literary society called *Al Rabita al Qalamiyyah* (The Pen Bond).

1923:   *The Prophet* is published, with immediate success. He begins a friendship with Barbara Young, who later becomes his new muse and editor.

1928:   *Jesus The Son of Man* is published.

1931:   Dies in a hospital in New York at the age of 48, due to cirrhosis of the liver. As was his wish, Gibran's body is transferred in 1932 to Lebanon and is buried in his native town of Bsharri. An old monastery is purchased, which becomes a museum to his memory.

These bare facts belie the complexity and turbulence of Kahlil Gibran's life, both inner and outer. As one of his biographers, Suheil Bushrui, writes:

> The more that has been written about Gibran, the more elusive the man himself has tended to become, as critics, friends, and biographers have built up a variety of unconnected pictures. Gibran himself is partly to blame. He wrote very little about his own life and in recurrent moments of insecurity and "vagueness," particularly during his first years of recognition, often fabricated or embellished his humble origins and troubled background. This self-perpetuation of his myth—a tendency followed by other literary figures such as Yeats and Swift—was not intellectual dishonesty, but a manifestation of the poetic mind's desire to create its own mythology. (Bushrui, 1998).

A good online biography can be found at the website of the Gibran National Committee: *www.gibrankhalilgibran.org*.

As Bushrui notes, the many biographies and biographical studies of Gibran do not agree on many points. They are very much like the different voices presented in Gibran's book *Jesus The Son of Man*, each reporting various facets of a person who embraced both the highs and lows, the lights and shadows of a fully human life.

A selection of the biographies and collections of Gibran's letters is below.

Bushrui, S., and J. Jenkins. (1998). *Kahlil Gibran: Man and Poet*. Oxford: Oneworld.

Bushrui, S., and S. H. al-Kuzbari (eds. and trans.), (1995). *Gibran: Love Letters*. Oxford: Oneworld.

Gibran, J. and K. Gibran. (1974). *Kahlil Gibran: His Life and World*. Boston: New York Graphic Society.

Gibran, J. and K. Gibran. (2017). *Kahlil Gibran: Beyond Borders*. (Updated version of the 1974 book). Northampton, MA: Interlink Books.

Hilu, V. (1972). *Beloved Prophet: The Love Letters of Kahlil Gibran and Mary Haskell and Her Private Journal.* New York: Alfred Knopf.

Naimy, M. (1950). *Kahlil Gibran: A Biography.* New York: Philosophical Library.

Waterfield, R. (1998). *Prophet: The Life and Times of Kahlil Gibran.* New York: St. Martin's Press.

Young, B. (1945). *This Man from Lebanon: A Study of Kahlil Gibran.* New York: Alfred Knopf.

KAHLIL GIBRAN'S LITTLE BOOK OF SECRETS

About the Editor

Neil Douglas-Klotz, PhD is a renowned writer in the fields of Middle Eastern spirituality and the translation and interpretation of the ancient Semitic languages of Hebrew, Aramaic, and Arabic. Living in Scotland, he directs the Edinburgh Institute for Advanced Learning and for many years was cochair of the Mysticism Group of the American Academy of Religion.

A frequent speaker and workshop leader, he is the author of several books. His books

Photo by William A. Matheiu

on the Aramaic spirituality of Jesus include *Prayers of the Cosmos, The Hidden Gospel, Original Meditation: The Aramaic Jesus and the Spirituality of Creation,* and *Blessings of the Cosmos.* His books on a comparative view of "native" Middle Eastern spirituality include *Desert Wisdom: A Nomad's Guide to Life's Big Questions* and *The Tent of Abraham* (with Rabbi Arthur Waskow and Sr. Joan Chittister). His books on Sufi spirituality include *The Sufi Book of Life: 99 Pathways of the Heart for the Modern Dervish* and *A Little Book of Sufi Stories.* His biographical collections of the works of his Sufi teachers include *Sufi Vision and Initiation* (Samuel L. Lewis) and *Illuminating the Shadow* (Moineddin Jablonski). He has also written a mystery novel set in the first century C.E. Holy Land entitled *A Murder at Armageddon.*

For more information about his work, see the website of the Abwoon Network *www.abwoon .org* or his Facebook page *https://www.facebook .com/AuthorNeilDouglasKlotz/.*

Hampton Roads
Publishing Company

. . . for the evolving human spirit

Hampton Roads Publishing Company publishes books on a variety of subjects, including spirituality, health, and other related topics.

For a copy of our latest trade catalog, call (978) 465-0504 or visit our distributor's website at *www.redwheelweiser.com*. You can also sign up for our newsletter and special offers by going to *www.redwheelweiser.com/newsletter/*.